SHADOW OF HEAVEN

 Poems

SHADOW OF HEAVEN

 Poems

ELLEN BRYANT VOIGT

W. W. NORTON & COMPANY

NEW YORK • LONDON

For information about permission to reproduce selections from this book, write to
Permissions, W. W. Norton & Company, Inc., 500 Fifth Avenue, New York, NY 10110

The text and display of this book are composed in Futura Light and Granjon
Composition by Adrian Kitzinger
Manufacturing by Courier Westford
Book design by BTDnyc
Production manager: Julia Druskin

ISBN 0-393-04147-6

W. W. Norton & Company, Inc., 500 Fifth Avenue, New York, N.Y. 10110
www.wwnorton.com

W. W. Norton & Company Ltd., Castle House, 75/76 Wells Street, London W1T 3QT

1 2 3 4 5 6 7 8 9 0

for Joan

CONTENTS

ACKNOWLEDGMENTS

I am grateful to the journals in which many of these poems
appeared previously, some under other titles: *DoubleTake,
Five Points, Ploughshares, River City, Slate, The Atlantic Monthly,
The Kenyon Review, The New Virginia Review, The New
Breadloaf Anthology, The Southern Review, The Threepenny
Review, The Yale Review,* and *TriQuarterly.* Thanks also to
the Lila Wallace–Reader's Digest Foundation for its support,
to J. D. McClatchy, for extracting from me the translations
of Horace, and to Agha Shahid Ali, for insisting that I write
a ghazal.

"Practice" is for Steve Orlen; "The Art of Distance, 4" is
for Fran; "Dooryard Flower" is in memory of Tom Moore.

... though what if Earth
Be but the shadow of Heaven, and things therein
Each to other like, more than on Earth is thought?

Paradise Lost

WINTER FIELD

LARGESSE

Aix-en-Provence

Banging the blue shutters—night-rain;
and a deep gash opened in the yard.
By noon, the usual unstinting sun
but also wind, the olive trees gone silver,
inside out, and the slender cypresses,
like women in fringed shawls, hugging themselves,
and over the rosemary hedge the pocked fig
giving its purple scrota to the ground.

What was it had made me sad? At the market,
stall after noisy stall, melons, olives,
more fresh herbs than I could name, tomatoes
still stitched to the cut vine, the soft
transparent squid shelved on ice; also,
hanging there beside the garlic braids,
meek as the sausages: plucked fowl with feet.

Under a goose-wing, I had a violent dream.
I was carrying a baby and was blind,
or blinded on and off, the ledge I walked
blanking out long minutes at a time.
He'd flung a confident arm around my neck.
A spidery crack traversed his china skull.
Then it was not a ledge but a bridge, like a tongue.

From the window over my desk, I could look down
at the rain-ruined nest the *sangliers*
had scrabbled in the thyme, or up, to the bald
mountain in all the paintings. I looked up.
That's where one looks in the grip of a dream.

APPLE TREE

No choice for the apple tree.
And after the surgeon's chainsaw,
from one stubborn root

two plumes of tree now leaf
and even blossom, sky's
cool blue between them,

whereas on my left hand
not a single lifeline
but three deep equal

channels—
       O my soul,
it is not a small thing,
to have made from three

this one, this one life.

WINTER FIELD

The winter field is not
the field of summer lost in snow: it is
another thing, a different thing.

"We shouted, we shook you," you tell me,
but there was no sound, no face, no fear, only
oblivion—why shouldn't it be so?

After they'd pierced a vein and fished me up,
after they'd reeled me back they packed me under
blanket on top of blanket, I trembled so.

The summer field, sun-fed, mutable,
has its many tasks; the winter field
becomes its adjective.
                          For those hours
I was some other thing, and my body,
which you have long loved well,
did not love you.

THE OTHERS

Our two children grown, now
is when I think
of the others:

          two more times

the macrocephalic sperm battered
its blunt cell forward, rash
leap to the viscous egg—

                  marriage
from our marriage, earth and fire—
and what then,

             in the open

synapse from God's finger
to Adam's hand?

              The soul
sent back:

       our lucky
or unlucky lost, of whom
we never speak.

PRACTICE

To weep unbidden, to wake
at night in order to weep, to wait
for the whisker on the face of the clock
to twitch again, moving
the dumb day forward—

is this merely practice?
Some believe in heaven,
some in rest. *We'll float,*
you said. *Afterward*
we'll float between two worlds—

five bronze beetles
stacked like spoons in one
peony blossom, drugged by lust:
if I came back as a bird
I'd remember that—

until everyone we love
is safe is what you said.

HIMALAYA

Branches: wings: we sheltered in thick fir trees.
The cliff-face, as we'd asked, had furnished trees.

When your mother died, I dreamed the wild mountain
of the grave, its myrrh and milk, fur and fleece.

I know what my soul saw: the sky like silk
pulled through a ring, a flock of wind-slurred trees.

Those feathery evergreens were blue—didn't you
wear blue for luck at all her surgeries?

Calm came into the dream, unburdened as snow.
It sugared the rocks, the rock-encircled trees.

You had no need to dream her back: your many
kisses were locks against death's burglaries.

Regret came into the dream thankless as snow.
It floured God's black beard, it furred the trees.

There was no pile of stones, laid one by one
to mark the leaden anniversaries.

No beasts, no birds—snow fine as smoke, and the only
quickened shapes, behind that curtain, were trees.

Years past, a soul slipped by the stone I was.
On the windowpane, frost's rucked embroideries.

Root and branch: the year of fasting ends.
Outside: veiled sun, snow's layered silks, blurred trees.

Whose ghost is it, Shahid, feeds my grief-dream?
Whose loss, whose task, whose darkened nursery?

LESSON

Whenever my mother, who taught
small children forty years,
asked a question, she
already knew the answer.
"Would you like to" meant
you would. "Shall we" was
another, and "Don't you think."
As in, "Don't you think
it's time you cut your hair."

So when, in the bare room,
in the strict bed, she said
"You want to see?" her hands
were busy at her neckline,
untying the robe, not looking
down at it, stitches
bristling where the breast
had been, but straight at me.

I did what I always did:
not weep—she never wept—
and made my face a kindly
white-washed wall, so she
could write, again, whatever
she wanted there.

HIGH WINDS FLARE UP AND
THE OLD HOUSE SHUDDERS

The dead should just shut up. Already
they've ruined the new-plowed field:
it looks like a grave. Adjacent pine-woods,
another set of walls: in that dark room
a birch, too young to have a waist,
practices sway and bend, slope and give.
And the bee at vertical rest on the outside pane,
belly facing in, one jointed limb crooked
to its mouth, the mouth at work—
my lost friend, of course, who lifelong
chewed his cuticles to the quick. Likewise
Jane who calls from her closet of walnut and silk
for her widower to stroke her breasts, her feet,
although she has no breasts, she has no feet,
exacting pity in their big white bed.
The dead themselves are pitiless—
they keen and thrash, or they lodge
in your throat like a stone, or they descend
as spring snow, as late light, as light-struck dust
rises and descends—frantic for more, more of this earth,
more of its flesh, more death, oh yes, and a few more
thousand last vast blue cloud-blemished skies.

THE GARDEN, SPRING, THE HAWK

from Baton Rouge
to my sister in Virginia

I

Like a struck match: redbird, riding the wet
knuckle of the longest limb of the leafless water oak,
pitching glissandi over the myrtle trees. The yellow cat,
one paw leveraged out of the soggy grass, then another,
has nothing to do with this: too slow, too old.
Nor the night-stunned snakes under the log, a cluster of commas;
nor the cloistered vole, the wasp, the translucent lizard,
the spider's swaddle of gauze, waiting to quicken.
This hour belongs to the birds—where I am,
single ripe berry on the bush; where you are,
Cooper's hawk, on the rail fence, dressing her feathers;
and the indistinct domestics at their chores.

2

While the prodigal husband is still asleep,
and the half-grown child, also sleeping, breathes in and out
as if that were the dullest task—while the migraine
loosens its fist and the pulse slows, one
overeager chamber of the heart and one reluctant
pumping together, lifting the blood and its boats
across the locks,
                                    is it possible yet to sit
at the broad window, hands around a cup,
the furnace in a modest hum, and make your mind
the streaked, sweaty pane a rag rubs clear?
Tree: fence: frogpond the size of a tire: residual moon:
each a weight to hold the skull-flap down.

3

The very air voluptuous and droll,
sometimes wrung into mist or vertical rain, Tuesday
breezes of shifting magnitudes, diaphanous cloud,
by Wednesday afternoon unsullied sun
but not hot—the season at this latitude
seems coy,

       seems feminine, I nearly said,
a woman napping in a frothy gown, and credit
thinking it

       not to having been away so long,
or the multitude of songbirds, courting and throbbing,
or the slutty blossoming of shrubs, but coming back
at all:

     the country of one's origin
is always *she,* the ground beneath the plow,

4

and the Deep South a clearer paradigm
than where you live beside the Northern Gate:
or Carolina where I went to school among magnolias,
back row, far left, one more blank white face:

or the first hill at the junction of woods and field,
functional garden, random flowers unsolicited,
and beyond the redbrick house, houses we built
below the pines in the soft trash of the forest floor—
days, weeks, we colonized a wilderness; it needed that *we,*

and closed to both of us when you were twelve, thirteen.
Time to be groomed for the breathless hunt-and-run,
purse and title at the finish line.

5

As if I were the moss, D. said, electric

and dismayed. House behind us scaffolded and draped

for surgery, she was showing me those hanks of woeful hair

harvested from live oaks down the street and rehung here;

it lives on air, like the gray Confederate ghosts

she sleeps among. Long-married, transplant, more guest

than host, she has a forced-resilience look (like my friend C.,

divorced last year, her heart prised like a root

from its tight pocket).

           Scissors and trowel: saw and chisel:

D. hired someone to help her stay, to knock away a wall

and put in glass. Like yours: window over the table,

row of doors to bring the outside in.

6

A back paw lifts: *adagio:* unlike
Thursday's cat harassing squirrels, untiringly,
that sallied forth from a clipped hibiscus, motoring
into open lawn where the hungry and the anxious
gathered food—hurry, hurry, they saw it coming on,
then leapt to a tree. After a long pause, the peril
hustled a straight line back to wait by the hedge.
Up and down the tree the squirrels flickered.
One by one they hazarded the ground.
Like criminals they angled toward the bread, nonchalant—
but spastic, too, their rigid compact bodies
ratcheting toward the source, the tree, the cat.

7

Soft, sweet, fetching, idle, pliable—whose
ideal was that? And how should it fit a childhood
reaching under a chicken for an egg? Or grown sisters, come
with gardens on their heads, who, at the sink, uncorseted,
let loose high-pitched complaint and low burlesque
as they itemized the Women's Fellowship, assaying
pew by pew the match that each had made.

Took me years to like that company. Meanwhile,
little pitcher with brains, I could see the men
leaning against the Packard in the yard, smoking,
toeing the hard red dirt, analyzing crops and cash,
or politics and war, or—or what? The world.

8

The slim successive cars like vertebrae
trailing the primitive skull, the train pulls forward,
past other trains and disconnected engines, Janus-faced;
negotiates the network of spurs and switches,
a thicket of poles and wires, sheer brick canyons,
signal-flags of laundry; passes the cotton mill's windows'
blind blue grid, and picks up speed downhill

as the late-model coupe turns left at the edge of town.
Windows open. Maps unpleated across the dash.
Something loud, popular and brisk, on the radio.

Now solve for x: how long, midday, they'll travel
neck and neck beside the broadening river. . . .

9

Against the brown field, bare trees, the hawk
swivels her head: becomes a bird. Cousin to eagle and kite,
marked like the smaller male she mates for life,
all that's vivid kept to the underside,

she doesn't touch the bread, the scraps of meat
you leave for the crows—it's mistakes she's after,
reckless mole, fledgling in the grass. The kitten
stays inside, hare in its hole. And you:
you've also learned to be good at holding still.

Why does a thing so fierce need camouflage?
Cooper's hawk, chicken hawk—you've seen her fly:
short wing-beats, and then the long glide.

Like an unsheathed falcon to the falconer
you *flew,* at eighteen, to his outstretched arm.
Restricted, addictive plural:

               and with it, your one
vocation. Why so eager for received idea?
This was not an absence of ambition but the heart thrown
like a rubbed coin. . . .

             Harder now to wish, harder to choose,
something in you drained off, or worn away,
and not yet, in its place, a new resolve—

you said so, late last fall, under the dead
limbs of the largest dogwood in the yard:
I can't even imagine a different life.

And spaded in another dozen bulbs.

II

My beautiful capable daughter, far from home
where rocks outnumber blossoms, had this dream:

I'd planted the steep hillside behind the house,
mostly vegetables, and they were huge: my secret
was salt, in which the bell peppers thrived and fruited,
and lush tomatoes, flowers on the barn's south side,
the path down through them littered with purple roses
(only the clenched, introverted heads), I'd put them there,
purple her favorite so I knew she'd follow
the bend in the brook to the level field which was—
I'd planted this, too—a broad expanse of white lace,
web of froth and steel: wedding gown.

Again and again the low-slung campus cat
charged out and back entirely purposeful:
that is, mechanical: in fact, remote-controlled
by a pleasant, detached young man behind the hedge,
studying Caution versus Appetite.
Clipboard, stopwatch, food, known patch of grass—
for the foragers, a closed set: he was measuring
how near his subjects let the danger come
before they bolted for the tree. Although by then
I could see it wasn't a very plausible cat,
remnants of shag glued to a model car,
it was hard to feel superior to the squirrels.

13

The cardinal sings and sings: hunter's horn;
then, artillery. The round red door to its heart
is always open. And now the same song
from down the street, this time a mockingbird,
which, like the emperor's toy, can do it better.

How many generations did it take to cultivate, in us,
the marriage gene? Or, if we simply learned our lessons well,
didn't you see it, smell it, in that air:
to loathe change is to loathe life—

                         Nevermind.
What you want from me is only an ear. Meanwhile,
the carpenters have come in their rusted truck
(Echo also does this bird quite well).

Once, there was a king with two daughters.
The older girl, of course, would take the throne.
And so it was left to the other to be clever.

Lead lute for the Young and Foolish Virgins,
she rode her great blue ox across the moat;
having a thorn in its hoof, it *needed* a friend.

She underwent the seven grueling labors.
She wrote a symphony. She wrote checks home.
Next, a sweet boy's rescue from the tower.

She cut his hair, he baked her bread, and soon
they were lumbering magnolias coast to coast—
it's that spilt seed strewn out across the heavens.

15

In the grass a beetle takes a quarter-turn;

in a week a window where there'd been a wall.

My hosts, plural and solicitous, apologize for winter's

monochrome, despite the fluent azalea, hibiscus, camellia—

whole trees of that soft fabric—aggressive bird:

one hundred shades of red. And basting the yard's edge

like stitches for a hem, like string at the mouth of a purse,

like a threading pulse, the cat prowls half-blind

among the shrubs. The student, asked if he had named

his cat, answered fast and earnest: "Oh no.

This is science." Intending, perhaps, like the exile,

to keep a little distance from what we are.

THE ART OF DISTANCE

I

Wrinkle coming toward me in the grass—no,
fatter than that, rickrack, or the scallops a ruffle makes,
down to about the fourteenth vertebra. The rest of it: rod
instead of a coil.

                So I'd been wrong the afternoon before
when the dog, curious, eager to play and bored with me
as I harvested the edge of the raspberry thicket,
stalked it from the back stoop to the lip
of the bank and grabbed the tip
in her mouth and tossed it—
sudden vertical shudder
shoulder-level—

              wrong
to read survival in its cursive
spiraling back to the cellar window-well
where it had gathered field mice like a cat.
And now, if it meant to be heading for the brook,
it veered off-course, its blunt head raised
like a swimmer's in distress.

                    The functioning part
gave out just short of me, inside the shade
but not the bush; the damaged part,
two fingers thick, was torqued
pale belly up, sunstruck.
I left it where it was,

took the dog in, and for hours
watched, from the kitchen window, what seemed
a peeled stick, the supple upper body that had dragged it
now pointed away and occluded by the shade,
the uncut grass.
              My strict father
would have been appalled: not to dispatch
a uselessly suffering thing made me the same, he'd say,
as the man who, seeing a toad,
catatonic Buddha in its niche, wedged
within the vise of a snake's efficient mouth
clamped open for, then closing slowly down and over it,
bludgeoned them both with the flat side of a hoe.

For once I will accept my father's judgment.
But this had been my yard, my snake, old enemy
resident at the back side of the house. For hours,
the pent dog panting and begging, I watched
from the window, as from a tower wall,
until it vanished: reluctant arrow
aimed at where the berries
ripened and fell.

2

My father was an earth-sign and a stoic,
an eldest child, a steward, who took dominion
over the given world—at least, it seemed,
his hundred acres of it, pets we ate,
rabbits minced in the combine, inchling moths
torched in the crotch of the tree to save the peaches.
Scorned excess and complaint. Importuned, said
no, not, can't, never will.
                What didn't fit
was seeing him cry. He'd stand alone in the field
like a rogue pine that had escaped the scythe,
as he would stand beside the family graves,
a short important distance from the car
where we were hushed until the white flag
had been unpocketed, and he jangled his keys
and got back in, not ever looking at us,

not looking at the brisk instructive face
my mother used on clerks, on amputees.
This all happened long before my mother,
in charge of cheerfulness and world morale,
had lost a body-part and given up—
so it was never in response to her,
the way he wept, or equally the way

he moved through life, one hoof after another:
a sentimental man is singular,
still the boy whose mother's gone away.
The last full day of our last ritual visit—
he'd taken a turn already into the field—
what set him off was hearing the neighbor's gun.
She merely wanted the turtle out of her beans;

he hauled the carcass home, two feet wide,
a rock from the creek, and also elderly
if the shell's whorls correspond to xylem and phloem,
rings we'd count on the cut trunk of a tree.
"Tastes like chicken," he said, gathering
the saw, the maul, chisel, pliers, hatchet
he'd need to unhouse the body and chop it up.

No one wanted to help, or even watch,
except the child intent on the row of knives,
and the child changing her mind with a webbed foot's wave—
dinner was not quite dead—but shudders and tears
were weakness and wouldn't work, jokes wouldn't work
on temper alchemized from noun into verb
as my father pried the armored plates apart,

pale and sweating and silent. And never did he,
sun long gone down, once quit the bloody porch,
the bowl of the upper shell in shards, the entrails
bejeweled with flies, the beaked head, feet and tail
cast off into wet grass, until, at the screen,
holding a platter of meat, he might have been
the Queen's woodsman bringing back the heart.

I heated the oil until it spit at me,
dredged the pieces in flour as I would chicken,
flung them chunk by chunk into the pan.
When chewed undefeated lumps ringed even his dish,
he said I'd done the best I knew, not
naming the skill: deflecting sorrow and terror
into a steady fierceness, and aiming *that*.

3

They shaved the torso from behind the nape, across the shoulder
to the center chest, taking away exactly the noble ruff
and adjacent sable winter-thickened fur,

making, when she crouches at my feet, the joint and sinew
discernible under the startled skin,
as in those close-up photos from the Veldt,
as if she were hunched above a slack gazelle

(but when she's sleeping on her side, her neck, extended,
might be the slack gazelle's).

Fifty-seven stitches track from the spine,
inside the sheltering ridge of the collarbone,
down to where the trachea enters lung,
their puckered, punctuated seam gathering
what something split apart, some creature
cornered in the woods or field,

no trophy, no raw meat except her own, no carcass
pinioned now beneath her paws,
only the wretched quilt,
torn and stained—

an obedient, courteous dog, she is abashed to pee indoors,
  she doesn't squat, she stands with her head low,
    like a whipped horse, as the gush puddles the floor—

and even though (or because) mostly when I touch her it is
  to apply the many therapies prescribed, pills
    down her throat, hot compress on the draining wound,
  or to smooth the pallet of her lying-in,

she neither whimpers loudly nor draws back:

therefore, she seems not only dutiful
  but grateful, too, as though the touch conveyed
    a recognition; a bond
      if not of pain, indignity;
    compassion not for another but for oneself.

    Which makes my hand enact a tenderness.
Like the rough warm tongue that licks the weak one clean.

4

When you saw your father last, he was tied into a chair
with a soft sash: the nurses had parked him, nearly
weightless, near the window, in sunlight: the shook
filaments of fine white hair repelled

every bead of light as his tremorous head drooped on its stalk—
the whole stalk drooped, curving down and in, the chin
sank toward the concave chest, the arms were veined
sticks from the sleeves of the gown like a sack,

but his hands, delicate, unlined, *deliberate,* were reaching
forward as a small child might reach to stroke the warm
bright beam that struck his knees.
                              "Still a doc,"
the charge-nurse said behind you at the door,

"still wants to diagnose." Said: the knees sometimes show
how close death is. A puffiness? Or granulated skin?
You didn't ask, seeing the focused will he lived by,
the avid mind, take its scientific measure,

the tips of the fingers glossing both kneecaps, comparing
each to each? Or, to the many patients in his head?
The rest of the body barely moved, except its slow
declension, the labored breaths so slow

and far apart: as though to practice for the long deep dive
the great sea-creatures make, only matched in humans
by the held moments when its brain shuts down
in order that the infant be delivered.

5

After lunch, on the side porch,
the uncinched wooden leg in a muddy boot
stood by the edge of the bed. Freed from the second boot:
a full-length human leg, denim on white chenille. The other
stopped at a blunt substantial thigh. Its puckered stump,
facing me, looked like a face, or a fist.
I looked at it hard.

Four hands, three legs and half
a brain, my uncle said: what my grandmother
salvaged from the war—her brother's wounded sons,
sullen Ed with his limp, Grover hunched and simpering.
They worked the fields and in the barn, ate in her kitchen,
hair slick from washing up, like the hired hands.
When she said grace,

my grandmother said it standing,
bandaging her hand in her apron skirt
to lift the cast iron skillet out of its round hole
to the square table of men. Burn herself up, her daughters said,
on Sundays, visiting like me, and scolding my uncle,
but still she fed with her fingers the squat stove,
and her grown wards

chopped the wood and hauled it,

pumped water, hauled it, cut hay, hauled it, hauled

the pig and cow and chicken shit and stirred the flies.

You keep out of the barn, my uncle said, after he'd found me

rapt by what they'd found: thick braid hung from a beam—

two blacksnakes writhing there like a hot wire,

a lit fuse.

What else do you need to know?

That my uncle, who was the baby, who went to war

and came home whole, who had no children, had no brothers,

thereby got the farm, would sell the farm—my uncle brought home,

for Grover, a puppy that liked to sleep in my grandmother's lap

and lick her plate, dirty little dog

her daughters said;

and a slick red racing bike,

which was not, with its manual brakes, the joke you think:

Ed stretched his crutch on the rack of the handlebars, slued

the stiff leg out and pumped the other, his sly pleasure breaking

through perfected scorn, cruising the porch where I sat

hulling peas in a china bowl—sometimes

the world looks back.

6

The enormous world shimmering—
> then, in the magic glass, some of it,
>> guessed at, came clear.

Whereas my friend "in nature"
> takes his glasses *off* so he
>> "can think." When he says

he thinks with his body—body
> grown substantial over the years,
>> as has his thought—

I don't know what he means; or,
> if I do, I think thinking is not
>> the body's job,

that the body gets in the way.
> Our friendship feeds on argument.
>> Each of us

has one prominent eye:
> his the one on the right, for the left
>> side of the brain,

language and logic; but mine—
        wide and unforgiving—mine
                is the one on the left,

enlarged by superstition
        and music, like my father's more
                myopic eye.

Detachment is my friend's
        discovery, what he commends
                against despair.

And though my father claimed
        I never listen, of course I do:
                after all, who else

but the blind will lead the blind?
        And the years bring their own correction:
                to see a thing

one has to push it away.

7

What art, like money, does is dig things up,
so that each tree and bush has its plateau—
tufts of frond in palms five stories high;
the spare flamboyant tree that seeds in pods,
its bunched florets; frangipani trees
to sweeten the air, clusters of white blossoms
with yellow throats; the mangrove trees, from whose
dense canopies descend the branch-like roots,
serpentine; and close to the ground, hedges
of bougainvillea, odorless, origami,
sometimes two colors on a single branch—
all rescued from the wet interior,
its undivided green, its bamboo swamps,
its breadfruit, mango, cocoa, guava, plum,
its forests of nutmeg trees, of almond trees—

Nobody needs be hungry here, excepting
what they wants is meat, Carlton said
when you remarked an isolated goat,
skeletal, among papaya trees.
Carlton's Tours are in his Chevrolet
(tan '68 sedan, original clutch),

and Carlton, wearing a tie, means to please,
courtly, bluffing when he doesn't know,
although he knows the flora, and where to find
abandoned factories that once made rum,
and overgrown plantations, and also where
the aborigines last took their stand:
on a bare cliff, so that, having lost again,
they could, and did, fling themselves to the sea.

One needs, it seems, sufficient irony:
to see oneself and the island as from the clouds:
a speck on the back of a gecko turning brown
these weeks before the rains, as if to hide
from the gray square-headed bird, its needle-nose,
its white chest and belly and underwing
blazed blue as it skims the azure swimming pool.
Past some small blackbirds, and the doctor-bird,
black with a blue face, who works like a bee
the oleander bush; past the cheery
banana-quit, across powdery sand,
raked everyday; and past broad-leaved sea grapes,
squat trees outposted near a ruffling surf:

How are you today? she says, and you say
Thank you, fine, and how are you?, and she says
Not as fine as you, and she is right:
you could buy a room in the new hotel,
and she cannot afford the ferry off.
Want my pretty? she says, proffering
her grass baskets, loofahs still in their shells,
and bowls made from the gourds of a calabash tree,
which also serve—she models one—as hats.
Don't want to burn, she says, and even though
your skin has never been so white, so soft,
you tell her Not today, and look at the sea:

past riffling waves, past gulls cresting the tide
like boats, past sun-struck sails, a pencil line
divides dove gray and blue from navy blue,
partitioning the heavens from the earth.
And every day at dusk, released from under
the mangrove's raised umbrella, that cupped hand
overturned and pouring out, bats come
to reattach us—not with the tiny stitches
trawlers make against the far horizon,
but like a loom's ratcheting shuttle, weaving
first a net, then a veil, and then a shroud.

DOORYARD FLOWER

HORACE: ODE I.xxxiv

Lazy in praising or praying to any god
and madly rational, a clever captain
cruising the open seas of human thought,

now I must bring my vessel full about,
tack into port and sail back out again
on the route from which I strayed. For the God of gods,

who slices through the storm with flashes of fire,
this time in a clear sky came thundering
with his storied horses and his chariot,

whereby the dumb dull earth and its fluttering streams—
and the River Styx, and the dreaded mouth of the cave
at the end of the world—were shaken. So the god

does have sufficient power after all
to turn the tables on both high and low,
the mighty humbled and the meek raised up—

with a swift hiss of her wings, Fortune swoops down,
pleased to place the crown on this one's head,
as she was pleased to snatch it away from that one.

PLAZA DEL SOL

This is a veterans' ward, here by the pool
in Florida, where every chaise is taken, every frame
stretched out to full extension, the bodies just removed
from cold storage, exposing to light and air
the wound, the scar, the birthmark's crushed grape,
contiguous chins undisguised by pearls,
pitted shoulders plumped or scapular, flesh
pleated under an upper arm, a vast loaf rising
out of the bathing bra, or chest collapsed
and belly preeminent, spine a trough
or a knotted vine climbing the broad cliff-wall.
Down from this pelvic arch five children came;
that suspicious mole, his mother kissed;
but who will finger such calves, their rosaries?
Here's a brace of ankles like water-balloons;
here's a set of toes shingled with horn.
Here is the man, prone, whose back is a pelt,
and the supine woman whose limbs are tinkertoys,
and the man whose tattooed eagle looks crucified,
and his brother with breasts, and his wife with none—
a woman tanned already, dried fruit arranged on a towel—
and her pale sister, seated, bosom piled in her lap,
oiling the lunar landscape of her thighs.
The hot eye over them all does not turn away

from bodies marooned inside loose colorful rags
or bursting their bandages there at the lip of the cave—
from ropy arms, or the heavy sack at the groin,
or the stone of the head—bodies mapped
and marbled, rutted, harrowed, warmed at last,
while everyone else has gone off into the sea.

ANTHROPOLOGY

The large dog sprawls in the road, remembering
his younger triumph over passing cars.
Here comes one now; it swerves, blares its horn,
and his littermate, a smaller quicker dog
trolling the suspect mole, slinks to the porch.
This fails to shame, or teach, or galvanize,
since he would rather be envied than admired—
he holds the road as lion would his rock,
walrus his floe.
           I knock on the windowpane;
he looks toward me, then turns his thick neck back
to look at the road. I knock again; he looks
at me, then heaves his body up, strolls
to the house with plausible irony: he's not
accountable, who woos whatever traffic
sidles past; whose sleep is comatose
and not disturbed, like hers, by the tic of the hunt;
whose head happens to reach to the willing hand—

my hand rubbing his crown, her currying tongue,
all of it costs him nothing. His one job?
To wag his tail when the Alpha Male comes home.
Meanwhile his busy sister patrols the yard,
chases after thunder out in the field,
bites midair in winter the snow-detritus
shuffling from the eaves—she knows she's a dog,
knows what dogs do:

              hope to please, and plunge.

A BRIEF DOMESTIC HISTORY

A lonely lonely man has come to our door.
He's looking for our friend, the bright penny
he pocketed years ago, who isn't here.
Widow Douglas when our friend was Huck,
and no one else to spend his worry on,
he settles in to wait. He loves to talk—
relieved to leave his solitude on the porch,
beast on a weak leash—and offers up
polished opinions on politics, neighbors, God,
the meal in the firkin: he's Emersonian,
but fond: with my teenaged son, my Bartleby
(whom he thinks is his Thoreau—i.e.,
smart, judgmental, passionate and spoiled),
he talks sports, its algebra. At last,

announced by a shredded muffler, Bright Penny
arrives, at twenty-five all optimistic
energy, lifting the lid off every pot.
Whitmanic, fresh from the world, full of the world,
he tows along a boy he plucked from the ditch
if only to remind him of himself;
they've come for my son, they lob the usual insults
at him, cuff him—the universal greeting—
and then, displacing Lonesome's *gravitas,*
the future commandeers the lit kitchen—
noisy, hungry, hairy, mammalian, gendered

but not entirely sexual, although
there is that carbonation in the air.

Which makes it seem it's the older wounded man
who's Whitman, trying to redirect his need.
Which means the one whose company he seeks,
grown thoughtless from self-reliance, is Emerson,
this time the younger, not afraid of Walt
though distant, proud, as someone's son might be.
So here's Walt/Waldo, abject at forty-eight,
and Waldo/Walt, magnetic at twenty-five,
something passing between them like a wire.
Or maybe an absence, a missing tether, the wire
loose on the ground. Which makes them, all of them, boys,

these two, and of course the even younger two,
my husband, also, just coming in from his lab,
redolent of the power the others covet
thus dismiss—all of them jousting and chafing,
each with his facts, each with his partial story,
none now willing to be seen as ever
odd or sad or lonely, foolish or frightened,
who're gathered at America's long oak table,
ready to fix whatever might be broken,
because I make great soup, great apple pie.

LONG MARRIAGE

Forward his numb foot, back
her foot, his chin on her head,
her head on his collarbone,

during those marathons
between wars, our vivid
Dark Times, each dancer holds

the other up so he,
as the vertical heap barely
moves yet moves, or she,

eyes half-lidded, unmoored,
can rest. Why these, surviving
a decimated field?

More than a lucky fit—
not planks planed from the same
oak trunk but mortise and tenon—

it is the yoke that makes
the pair, that binds them to
their blind resolve, two kids

who thought the world was burning
itself out, and bet
on a matched disregard

for the safe and the sad—*Look,*
one hisses toward the flared
familiar ear, *we've come*

this far, this far, this far.

AUTUMN IN THE YARD
WE PLANTED

Whoever said that I should count on mind?
Think it through, think it up—now that I know so much,
what's left to think is the unthinkable.

And the will has grown too tired to stamp its foot.
It sings a vapid song, it dithers and mopes,
it takes its basket to the marketplace,
like a schoolgirl in her best dress, and watches
others ask outright for what they want—
how do they know what they want?—and haul it away,
the sweet, the dull, the useless and the dear.

A maudlin, whimpering song: in which I lament
my own children, scything their separate paths
into the field, one with steady strokes,
one in a rage. We taught them that. And,
not to look back: at the apple tree, first
to shatter its petals onto the clipped grass,
or the slovenly heads of the russet peonies,

or even that late-to-arrive pastel, all stalk
with a few staggered blossoms, meadow rue—
though surely they could see it from where they are.

LAST LETTER

A proper interval, and then
you must love twice as hard, and fast.

I dreamed it years ago, more
a feeling than a plotline: I was

invisible and watched it all:
everything the same, the house

our house, children, the shape of the days.
It was summer in the dream, late

dinner on the screened porch, so what
if another woman made the soup,

the salad. I also watched by the bed—
you stroked her with your broad left hand—

and watching, thought: she ought to be glad
I'd broken you in. And felt a rueful

tenderness. And thought, or felt,
she looks like me—and so the dream

pleased me with its flattery.
But now I think, better what

you didn't have, and recommend
pliant and serene, perhaps

a little blithe. That bright morning
after the dream, the dream rushed back

only when I had stood, unthinking,
in the hot shower, and at its touch,

wept, like blown glass shattering,
before the narrative, remembered,

told me why. My weeping's done.
You will have the harder task,

it's true, but don't you see? Your need
will be your tribute, my legacy.

HORACE: ODE I.xxxvii

Nunc est bibendum . . .

Now it's time to drink, now loosen your shoes
and dance, now bring around elaborate couches
and set the gods a feast, my friends! Before,

the time wasn't right to pour the vintage wines,
not while that queen and her vile brood of advisors,
dizzy with desire and drunk on luck,
were busy in deluded plots against us.

What sobered her up was seeing her fleet on fire—
hardly a ship survived—nightmare she woke to
sending her fleeing, flying, from our shores,

Caesar at the oars in close pursuit—
the way the hawk harasses the helpless dove,
or the hunter the hare in the snow-packed open field—
intent on dragging the monster back in chains.

And yet the death that she resolved was grand:
a woman who did not shrink from the drawn blade,
who did not try to slip away and hide,

she looked straight at the palace now in ruins,
her face composed, and without blinking took
into her arms the scaly venomous snakes
in order to drink each drop of their black wine,

and by that cup this woman of such fierce pride
made the triumph hers: that she would die
not as a slave, and not as someone's prize.

WHAT I REMEMBER
OF LARRY'S DREAM OF YEATS

A roomful of writers, three on the couch a cat
had pissed on, others clustered like animated trees,
Shahid benched at the melodiophobic piano
Reg had played while Deb and Karen sang;
and centered, under the fixture overhead, Larry,
pleated around a straight-backed chair, not drinking
then, not doing dope, his face above the mustache open
for company—although I heard him tell the dream
in North Carolina, after he moved to Virginia,

he'd dreamed it long before in Salt Lake City.
"Things not going very well," he summarized,
hurrying to what would make us laugh: him alone
and broke and barely hanging on, Strand advising
"'Buy silk sheets.'" I've forgotten whether or not
he did, whether or not the stained mattress
had been sheathed in silk, because he so expertly
buried for us that bed in papers, notebooks, volumes
underlined, low mound of the written word

as erudite, disheveled as Larry was,
taking a turn in the light of our attention, T-shirt
even though it was winter, distressed gray hair.
"In the midst of this" (here he lit another smoke),
"I'd been preparing for my class on Yeats," days, nights
on guided tours of the Variorum and *A Vision;*
also in the layers, the *L.A. Times,* manuscripts of poems
(his students' and his own), clean and dirty laundry,
letters, bills, an opened bag of chips.

Both white feet splayed flat on the splintered floor,
forearms on his knees, he leaned forward, maybe
to give this part some shoring-up, since labor
ran counter to his irony, his off-the-cuff,
his disaffected style—but didn't he know we knew
intelligence as restless and large as his
needs feeding from time to time? (What did Dobyns say:
a billion who ought to die before Larry did?) Besides,
he looked so much like a caught thief coming clean,

none of us doubted he had read it all,

everything on Yeats, and fell asleep, and Yeats

stopped by, wearing a white suit. He'd come to retrieve

a last still-undiscovered poem, which he happened to keep

in Utah, in a locked drawer in Larry's room—just then

the kitchen howled and hooted, as if Larry

had also been in *there,* doing Justice, teacher

he loved, as an ice-cream man. Here's when Dr. Orlen

entered the room, stirring a short Scotch-rocks,

and Larry double-stitched: "Yeats in white,

pointing at my notes: 'Why do you bother with *that?*'"

Pause. Larry stared at Tony, next at me, the three of us

sharing the one ashtray, his eyebrows up, accents

acute et grave, like facing, aggressive bears:

"'Passion,' Yeats said, 'is all that matters in poetry.'"

Trawling the line to see if we would bite,

he leaned back in the chair, chair on its hind legs,

his legs straight out, his mouth a puckered seam.

In the dream Yeats turned away, as we ourselves
were starting to turn away now from the dream, to reach
for another fistful of chips or Oreos, another humiliation
from the Poetry Wars, another sensual or shapely thing
to throw at loneliness or grief, like what I'll hear
from Mary Flinn, how, when Richmond's ROBINSON'S REMOVAL
came for the body, days still undiscovered on the floor,
to wrestle it like a sodden log out to the hearse,
they swaddled it first in a scarlet velvet tarp,

then aimed for the stairs, headlong, the tapered end
under the arm of a ravaged small thin old black man
(that's Robinson), his doughy-bosomed lieutenant at the helm,
and Mary, foot of the stairs and looking up, expecting
Larry to break loose any minute, tumble forward—
the kind of punchline we were avid for
that evening in Swannanoa with good friends
(was Heather there? was Lux fanning the fire?) when Larry
pulled himself upright and dropped his voice

as Yeats paused at the door in a white silk suit:
ancient, graveled, this was the voice of the caged sibyl,
shriveled the size of a flea, when he read, from his long poem,
her song, "I want to die;" and saying now, as Yeats, "'Passion
is also all that matters in *life*.'"

So weren't the dream,
and the telling of the dream, more lanky shrewd inclusive
Levis poems, like those in his books, those he left
in the drawer? If he comes to get them, let him come
in his usual disguise: bare feet, black clothes.

DOORYARD FLOWER

Because you're sick I want to bring you flowers,
flowers from the landscape that you love—
because it is your birthday and you're sick
I want to bring outdoors inside,
the natural and wild, picked by my hand,
but nothing is blooming here but daffodils,
archipelagic in the short green
early grass, erupted
bulbs planted decades before we came,
the edge of where a garden once was kept
extended now in a string of islands I straddle
as in a fairy tale, harvesting,
not taking the single blossom from a clump
but thinning where they're thickest, tall-stemmed
from the mother patch, dwarf to the west, most
fully opened, a loosened whorl,
one with a pale spider luffing her thread,
one with a slow beetle chewing the lip, a few
with what's almost a lion's face, a lion's mane,
and because there is a shadow on your lungs, your liver,
and elsewhere, hidden,
some of those with delicate green
streaks in the clown's ruff (*corolla*—
actually made from adapted leaves), and more

right this moment starting to unfold, I've gathered
my two fists full, I carry them like a bride,
I am bringing you the only glorious thing
in the yards and fields between my house and yours,
none of the tulips budded yet, the lilac
a sheaf of sticks, the apple trees
withheld, the birch unleaved—
it could still be winter here, were it not
for green dotted with gold, but you won't wait
for dogtoothed violets, trillium under the pines,
and who could bear azaleas, dogwood, early profuse rose
of somewhere else when you're assaulted here, early May,
not any calm narcissus, orange *corona*
on scalloped white, not even its slender stalk
in a fountain of leaves, no stiff cornets of the honest
jonquils, gendered parts upthrust in brass and cream:
just this common flash in anyone's yard,
scrambled cluster of petals
crayon-yellow, as in a child's drawing of the sun,
I'm bringing you a sun, a children's choir, host
of transient voices, first bright
splash in the gray exhausted world, a feast
of the dooryard flower we call butter-and-egg.